ALTO SAX

AUDIO ACCESS INCLUDED

PLAYBACK+
ed • Pitch • Balance • Loop

Disney Movie Hits

To access audio visit:
www.halleonard.com/mylibrary

Enter Code
6594-5765-4682-5046

ISBN 978-1-634-00095-9

Disney characters and artwork © Disney Enterprises, Inc.

WALT DISNEY MUSIC COMPANY
WONDERLAND MUSIC COMPANY, INC.

DISTRIBUTED BY

7777 W. BLUEMOUND RD. P.O. BOX 13819 MILWAUKEE, WI 53213

Visit Hal Leonard Online at
www.halleonard.com

BELLE

From Walt Disney's BEAUTY AND THE BEAST

Lyrics by HOWARD ASHMAN
Music by ALAN MENKEN

ALTO SAX

A WHOLE NEW WORLD

From Walt Disney's ALADDIN

Music by ALAN MANKEN
Lyrics by TIM RICE

ALTO SAX

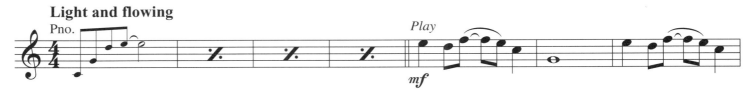

PRINCE ALI
From Walt Disney's ALADDIN

Lyrics by HOWARD ASHMAN
Music by ALAN MENKEN

ALTO SAX

GOD HELP THE OUTCASTS

From Walt Disney's THE HUNCHBACK OF NOTRE DAME

Music by ALAN MENKEN
Lyrics by STEPHEN SCHWARTZ

ALTO SAX

HAKUNA MATATA

From Walt Disney Pictures' THE LION KING

Music by ELTON JOHN
Lyrics by TIM RICE

ALTO SAX

BEAUTY AND THE BEAST

From Walt Disney's BEAUTY AND THE BEAST

Lyrics by HOWARD ASHMAN
Music by ALAN MENKEN

ALTO SAX

CRUELLA DE VIL

From Walt Disney's ONE HUNDRED AND ONE DALMATIANS

Words and Music by
MEL LEVEN

ALTO SAX

WHEN SHE LOVED ME

From Walt Disney Pictures' TOY STORY 2 – A Pixar Film

Music and Lyrics by
RANDY NEWMAN

ALTO SAX

KISS THE GIRL

From Walt Disney's THE LITTLE MERMAID

Lyrics by HOWARD ASHMAN
Music by ALAN MENKEN

ALTO SAX

IF I DIDN'T HAVE YOU

Walt Disney Pictures Presents
A Pixar Animation Studios Film MONSTERS, INC.

Music and Lyrics by
RANDY NEWMAN

ALTO SAX

GO THE DISTANCE

From Walt Disney Pictures' HERCULES

Music by ALAN MENKEN
Lyrics by DAVID ZIPPEL

ALTO SAX

CIRCLE OF LIFE

From Walt Disney Pictures' THE LION KING

Music by ELTON JOHN
Lyrics by TIM RICE

ALTO SAX

HAL•LEONARD INSTRUMENTAL PLAY-ALONG

Your favorite songs are arranged just for solo instrumentalists with this outstanding series. Each book includes a great full-accompaniment play-along CD so you can sound just like a pro! Check out **www.halleonard.com** to see all the titles available.

Disney Greats

Arabian Nights • Hawaiian Roller Coaster Ride • It's a Small World • Look Through My Eyes • Yo Ho (A Pirate's Life for Me) • and more.

___	00841934	Flute	$12.99
___	00841935	Clarinet	$12.95
___	00841936	Alto Sax	$12.95
___	00841937	Tenor Sax	$12.95
___	00841938	Trumpet	$12.95
___	00841939	Horn	$12.95
___	00841940	Trombone	$12.95
___	00841941	Violin	$12.99
___	00841942	Viola	$12.95
___	00841943	Cello	$12.95
___	00842078	Oboe	$12.95

Great Themes

Bella's Lullaby • Chariots of Fire • Get Smart • Hawaii Five-O Theme • I Love Lucy • The Odd Couple • Spanish Flea • and more.

___	00842468	Flute	$12.99
___	00842469	Clarinet	$12.99
___	00842470	Alto Sax	$12.99
___	00842471	Tenor Sax	$12.99
___	00842472	Trumpet	$12.99
___	00842473	Horn	$12.99
___	00842474	Trombone	$12.99
___	00842475	Violin	$12.99
___	00842476	Viola	$12.99
___	00842477	Cello	$12.99

Coldplay

Clocks • Every Teardrop Is a Waterfall • Fix You • In My Place • Lost! • Paradise • The Scientist • Speed of Sound • Trouble • Violet Hill • Viva La Vida • Yellow.

___	00103337	Flute	$12.99
___	00103338	Clarinet	$12.99
___	00103339	Alto Sax	$12.99
___	00103340	Tenor Sax	$12.99
___	00103341	Trumpet	$12.99
___	00103342	Horn	$12.99
___	00103343	Trombone	$12.99
___	00103344	Violin	$12.99
___	00103345	Viola	$12.99
___	00103346	Cello	$12.99

Popular Hits

Breakeven • Fireflies • Halo • Hey, Soul Sister • I Gotta Feeling • I'm Yours • Need You Now • Poker Face • Viva La Vida • You Belong with Me • and more.

___	00842511	Flute	$12.99
___	00842512	Clarinet	$12.99
___	00842513	Alto Sax	$12.99
___	00842514	Tenor Sax	$12.99
___	00842515	Trumpet	$12.99
___	00842516	Horn	$12.99
___	00842517	Trombone	$12.99
___	00842518	Violin	$12.99
___	00842519	Viola	$12.99
___	00842520	Cello	$12.99

Lennon & McCartney Favorites

All You Need Is Love • A Hard Day's Night • Here, There and Everywhere • Hey Jude • Let It Be • Nowhere Man • Penny Lane • She Loves You • When I'm Sixty-Four • and more.

___	00842600	Flute	$12.99
___	00842601	Clarinet	$12.99
___	00842602	Alto Sax	$12.99
___	00842603	Tenor Sax	$12.99
___	00842604	Trumpet	$12.99
___	00842605	Horn	$12.99
___	00842606	Trombone	$12.99
___	00842607	Violin	$12.99
___	00842608	Viola	$12.99
___	00842609	Cello	$12.99

Women of Pop

Bad Romance • Jar of Hearts • Mean • My Life Would Suck Without You • Our Song • Rolling in the Deep • Single Ladies (Put a Ring on It) • Teenage Dream • and more.

___	00842650	Flute	$12.99
___	00842651	Clarinet	$12.99
___	00842652	Alto Sax	$12.99
___	00842653	Tenor Sax	$12.99
___	00842654	Trumpet	$12.99
___	00842655	Horn	$12.99
___	00842656	Trombone	$12.99
___	00842657	Violin	$12.99
___	00842658	Viola	$12.99
___	00842659	Cello	$12.99

Movie Music

And All That Jazz • Come What May • I Am a Man of Constant Sorrow • I Believe I Can Fly • I Walk the Line • Seasons of Love • Theme from *Spider Man* • and more.

___	00842090	Clarinet	$10.95
___	00842092	Tenor Sax	$10.95
___	00842094	Horn	$10.95
___	00842095	Trombone	$10.95
___	00842096	Violin	$10.95
___	00842097	Viola	$10.95

TV Favorites

The Addams Family Theme • The Brady Bunch • Green Acres Theme • Happy Days • Johnny's Theme • Linus and Lucy • Theme from the Simpsons • and more.

___	00842079	Flute	$10.95
___	00842080	Clarinet	$10.95
___	00842081	Alto Sax	$10.95
___	00842082	Tenor Sax	$10.95
___	00842083	Trumpet	$10.95
___	00842084	Horn	$10.95
___	00842087	Viola	$10.95

Wicked

As Long As You're Mine • Dancing Through Life • Defying Gravity • For Good • I'm Not That Girl • Popular • The Wizard and I • and more.

___	00842236	Flute	$11.95
___	00842237	Clarinet	$11.99
___	00842238	Alto Saxophone	$11.95
___	00842239	Tenor Saxophone	$11.95
___	00842240	Trumpet	$11.99
___	00842241	Horn	$11.95
___	00842242	Trombone	$11.95
___	00842243	Violin	$11.95
___	00842244	Viola	$11.95
___	00842245	Cello	$11.95

FOR MORE INFORMATION, SEE YOUR LOCAL MUSIC DEALER, OR WRITE TO:

HAL•LEONARD CORPORATION

7777 W. BLUEMOUND RD. P.O. BOX 13819 MILWAUKEE, WI 53213

0915